Alfred's

INSTRUMENTAL
PLAY-ALONG

CD+ INSIDE

Trombone

Level 1

EASY
CLASSIC THEMES
INSTRUMENTAL SOLOS

Arranged by Bill Galliford

Audio recordings created by
Galliford and Ethan Neuburg
Produced by Bill Galliford

© 2018 Alfred Music
All Rights Reserved. Printed in USA.

ISBN-10: 1-4706-3990-4 (Book & CD)
ISBN-13: 978-1-4706-3990-7 (Book & CD)

Alfred

Contents

mp3 CD Track

Image credits: *Portrait of Antonio Vivaldi* attributed to François Morellon la Cave courtesy of Driante70/PD • *Portrait of Ludwig van Beethoven when composing the Missa Solemnis* by Joseph Karl Stieler courtesy of Denniss/PD • *Foto ANton Dvorak in 1868* courtesy of Anoniem/PD • *Johann Christoph Pachelbel portrait, circa 1748* courtesy of Raul654/PD • *Pjotr I. Tschaikowski* by Nikolai Dmitriyevich Kuznetsov courtesy of Dmitry Rozhkov/PD • *First performance of Nutcracker in Mariinsky Theater* (anonymous) courtesy of Alex Bakharev/PD • *Portrait of Johann Sebastian Bach* by Elias Gottlob Haussmann courtesy of Jbarta/PD • *Manuscript for Notebook for Anna Magdalena Bach (1725)* courtesy of BachFan/CC-BY-4.0 • *Portrait of Ludwig van Beethoven* by Carl Jaeger courtesy of Library of Congress, LC-USZ62-29499/PD • *Johannes Brahms* courtesy of Loveless/PD • *Score for Pirithoüs* by Jean-Joseph Mouret courtesy of Bassani/CC-BY-4.0 • *Portrait of Joseph Haydn* by Thomas Hardy courtesy of Meidosensei/PD • *Skuespilleren Henrik Klausen i Peer Gynt av Henrik Ibsen. Fra uroppførelsen ved Christiania Theater 1876* by Severin Worm-Petersen courtesy of Norsk Teknisk Museum/CC-BY-4.0 • *Edvard Grieg portrait* by K. Nyblin courtesy of Bergen Public Library/PD • *Poster for an American production of Georges Bizet's Carmen* by Liebler & Maass Lith., New York (ca. 1896) courtesy of Library of Congress, LC-USZC4-8298/PD • *Portrait of Georges Bizet* by Étienne Carjat courtesy of Jappalang/PD • *1874 playbill from a French production of Orpheus in the Underworld* by Jules Cheret courtesy of Urdangaray/PD • *Jacques Offenbach* by Nadar courtesy of Adam Cuerden/PD

Spring

(from *The Four Seasons*)

Antonio Vivaldi
(1678–1741)

"Spring" was written as part of a group of four violin concerti titled *The Four Seasons* by Italian composer Antonio Vivaldi. Each concerto musically depicts one of the four seasons: spring, summer, autumn, and winter.

The Four Seasons represents one of the earliest examples of *program music*—instrumental music that tells a story or evokes imagery. During performances of program music, audiences were often provided text in their program notes to describe the story or scene of that piece. In the Romantic era, this became a very popular idea, with composers like Hector Berlioz and Richard Strauss contributing famous examples.

In *The Four Seasons*, Vivaldi included sonnets that explained how to play the piece and what to listen for as an audience. After the grand entrance of spring in the first movement of the "Spring" concerto, the birds sing and the creeks peacefully flow. After, a storm comes and the thunder rolls.

Here is the sonnet that accompanies the first movement of the "Spring" concerto:

Springtime is upon us.
The birds celebrate her return with festive song,
and murmuring streams are
softly caressed by the breezes.
Thunderstorms, those heralds of Spring, roar,
casting their dark mantle over heaven,
Then they die away to silence,
and the birds take up their charming songs once more.

SPRING

(from *The Four Seasons*)

Composed by
ANTONIO VIVALDI
Arranged by BILL GALLIFORD

Track 2: Demo
Track 3: Play-Along

Vivace (♩ = 160)
(Tempo click)

Ode to Joy

("Choral Theme" from *Symphony No. 9*)

Ludwig van Beethoven
(1770–1827)

Born in Bonn, Germany, Ludwig van Beethoven is one of the important composers in history, and his final symphony, *Symphony No. 9*, is one of the most notable pieces of music. Famously, Beethoven included vocalists in the final movement of this symphony, marking the first time that had ever been done. The main musical theme in the final movement is known as "Ode to Joy."

German writer and historian Friedrich Schiller wrote the poem "Ode to Joy" in 1785 and revised it in 1808. Beethoven used this text as the basis of the finale of his symphony, which he completed in 1824. Through time, the main melody in the finale became known by the name of Schiller's poem.

"Ode to Joy" has been used for countless purposes and occasions. In the 1970s, it was chosen as the "Anthem of Europe" by the Council of Europe, later becoming the official anthem of the European Union.

ODE TO JOY
("Choral Theme" from *Symphony No. 9*)

Track 4: Demo
Track 5: Play-Along

Composed by
LUDWIG VAN BEETHOVEN
Arranged by BILL GALLIFORD

Largo

(from *Symphony No. 9,* "New World")

Antonín Dvořák
(1841–1904)

In 1892, Czech composer Antonín Dvořák moved to New York City to teach at the National Conservatory of Music of America and to explore American music, particularly that of African-Americans and Native Americans. When the New York Philharmonic commissioned him to write a piece, he used his new discoveries as inspiration for his *Symphony No. 9,* commonly called the *New World Symphony.*

The National Conservatory of Music in America was unique in its time because it welcomed both men and women, and people of various races and cultures. While teaching there, Dvořák befriended African-American composer Harry T. Burleigh, who sang traditional spirituals for him. Burleigh's spirituals inspired the beautiful theme of "Largo," the second movement of Dvořák's *New World Symphony.*

Dvořák was also inspired by the landscapes of America. It is often said that he meant for the *New World Symphony* to convey America's "wide open spaces."

Canon in D

Johann Pachelbel
(1653–1706)

Canon in D, commonly known as *Pachelbel's Canon*, was almost forgotten, as German composer Johann Pachelbel's music went out of style after his death and wasn't rediscovered until the 20th century. It has now become one of the most well-known and beloved compositions in music. Among other things, it is one of the most popular pieces of music for wedding ceremonies.

A *canon* is a composition based on layers of the same melody overlapping with each other. The song "Row, Row, Row Your Boat" is a type of canon known as a *round*. In a round, one singer or group of singers sings a melody, then a second singer or group of singers joins in by singing the melody from the beginning while the original melody continues. This can keep going with more and more layers added. *Canon in D* uses a similar approach but with an additional part—a repeated bass line and chord accompaniment that continues throughout.

Canon in D has had a wide-reaching influence on pop music. Numerous music acts, including Pet Shop Boys, The Farm, Green Day, Oasis, Vitamin C, and Coolio, have borrowed the piece's iconic chord progression to create hit songs.

CANON IN D

Track 8: Demo
Track 9: Play-Along

Composed by
JOHANN PACHELBEL
Arranged by BILL GALLIFORD

Andante (♩ = 65)

molto rit.

Dance of the Sugar Plum Fairy

(from *The Nutcracker*)

Peter Ilyich Tchaikovsky
(1840–1893)

One of the most celebrated ballets is Russian composer Peter Ilyich Tchaikovsky's Christmastime classic *The Nutcracker*. It tells the story of a girl named Clara, whose toy nutcracker comes to life, turns into a prince, and takes her to his kingdom. While Clara is in the prince's kingdom, the Sugar Plum Fairy performs a famous dance, known as the "Dance of the Sugar Plum Fairy," for her.

During a visit to France in 1891, Tchaikovsky encountered a newly invented instrument known as the *celesta*. He wrote that the instrument was "midway between a tiny piano and a glockenspiel, with a divinely wonderful sound." He kept his discovery a secret, so that he could be the first in Russia to use it. It is the celesta that creates the beautiful bell-like sound that characterizes this piece, and the celesta has since become a regular instrument in most major orchestras.

The Nutcracker is unique in that the Sugar Plum Fairy is the *prima ballerina*, the chief dancer in a ballet, but she doesn't have her big solo until this dance, which is near the end of the ballet.

DANCE OF THE SUGAR PLUM FAIRY

(from *The Nutcracker*)

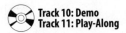

Track 10: Demo
Track 11: Play-Along

Composed by
PETER ILYICH TCHAIKOVSKY
Arranged by BILL GALLIFORD

Trepak

(from *The Nutcracker*)
(Russian Dance)

First performance of *The Nutcracker* in Mariinsky Theater

Peter Ilyich Tchaikovsky
(1840–1893)

Peter Ilyich Tchaikovsky visited Ukraine, which was part of Russia at the time, regularly throughout his life and composed several pieces of music there. Ukrainian folk music is the main source of inspiration for "Trepak," which is based on a traditional Ukrainian dance known as the *Tropak*.

In the second act of Tchaikovsky's ballet *The Nutcracker*, Clara, the heroine, is honored with sweets from around the world: chocolate from Spain, coffee from Arabia, tea from China, and candy canes from Russia. All the sweets perform a dance to represent their part of the world, with the candy canes dancing to "Trepak" (also called "Russian Dance").

Despite being very short, "Trepak" has become one of Tchaikovsky's best-known compositions. It can be heard in numerous television shows, video games, and films, including Walt Disney's *Fantasia*, where flowers perform this traditional dance.

TREPAK
(from *The Nutcracker*)
(Russian Dance)

Composed by
PETER ILYICH TCHAIKOVSKY
Arranged by BILL GALLIFORD

Track 12: Demo
Track 13: Play-Along

*An easier alternative note has been provided.

Air on the G String

(from *Orchestral Suite No. 3 in D Major*)

Johann Sebastian Bach
(1685–1750)

Bach was born in Eisenach, Germany and worked throughout Germany during his lifetime. Compared to other notable composers of the Baroque era, Johann Sebastian Bach wrote very few pieces for orchestra. His four *Orchestral Suites* are among the few pieces of orchestral music he wrote, and "Air on the G String" can be found in the third orchestral suite.

Bach's *Orchestral Suite No. 3 in D Major* was composed for trumpets, timpani, oboes, strings, and *basso continuo* (the bass line and harmonic accompaniment). The second movement, "Air," only featured strings and basso continuo. In the late 19th century, German violinist August Wilhelmj wrote an arrangement of "Air" for violin and piano. In it, Wilhelmj transposed the melody down a major ninth so that it can be played entirely on the violin's lowest string (G). When Wilhelmj notated the score, he wrote *auf de G-Saite* ("on the G string") over the violin part. The piece has since become known as "Air on the G String."

Airs were songs for lute and voice in the 16th century. By the 18th century, composers like Bach and George Frideric Handel used the term to identify a piece of instrumental music that is song-like.

AIR ON THE G STRING
(from *Orchestral Suite No. 3 in D Major*)

Composed by
JOHANN SEBASTIAN BACH
Arranged by BILL GALLIFORD

Track 14: Demo
Track 15: Play-Along

Minuet in G

(from *Notebook for Anna Magdalena Bach*)

"Minuet in G" as it is found in the *Notebook for Anna Magdelena Bach*

Christian Petzold
(1677–1733)

In 1722 and 1725, Johann Sebastian Bach presented his wife with two manuscript notebooks, both known today as *Notebook for Anna Magdalena Bach*. While the 1722 book contained only pieces by J. S. Bach, the 1725 book contained pieces by various composers. One of the pieces in the 1725 book is the "Minuet in G."

Anna Magdalena notated most of the music in the 1725 notebook herself, while J. S. Bach and a few others contributed entries. Many of the pieces in the book did not include composer credits: some were composed by J. S. Bach, some were popular songs of the time, and some were written by other composers. Up until 1970, "Minuet in G" was incorrectly credited to J. S. Bach, but it is now agreed among researchers that the piece was written by a contemporary of Bach's named Christian Petzold.

In 1965, "Minuet in G" was adapted into a pop song, called "A Lover's Concerto," by songwriters Sandy Lizner and Denny Randal, and recorded by the girl group The Toys. It became a hit in both the U.S. and the U.K.

MINUET IN G
(from *Notebook for Anna Magdalena Bach*)

Composed by
CHRISTIAN PETZOLD
Arranged by BILL GALLIFORD

Track 16: Demo
Track 17: Play-Along

Für Elise

Ludwig van Beethoven
(1770–1827)

Composer Ludwig van Beethoven began his musical career as a piano virtuoso, so it comes as no surprise that some of his best-known pieces are among the most celebrated piano music ever written. One of these classics is "Für Elise" (German for "For Elise").

The identity of "Elise" has been the subject of a lot of research and remains a mystery today. One commonly accepted theory is that the dedication was transcribed incorrectly in the first version, and that it was supposed to be called "Für Therese." Beethoven is thought to have had an unrequited romantic interest in a woman named Therese Malfatti, and it is suspected he wrote the piece for her. Another theory is "Elise" refers to a soprano singer named Elisabeth Röckel, who was the wife of another composer and friend of Beethoven's, Johann Nepomuk Hummel. Röckel was the first to play the lead in Beethoven's only opera, *Fidelio*. A letter has been uncovered in which Beethoven addresses her as "Elise."

Though it is one of Beethoven's most popular pieces, "Für Elise" was not published until 40 years after he died. German music scholar Ludwig Nohl discovered, transcribed, and published it in 1867.

FÜR ELISE

Track 18: Demo
Track 19: Play-Along

Composed by
LUDWIG VAN BEETHOVEN
Arranged by BILL GALLIFORD

Wiegenlied: Guten Abend, Gute Nacht (Good Evening, Good Night)

(Brahms' Lullaby)

Johannes Brahms
(1833–1897)

German composer Johannes Brahms is one of the most influential and important composers in history, writing for nearly every genre available to him. One of his most recognizable melodies is the tune widely known as "Brahms Lullaby." The full name of Brahms' vocal piece is *Wiegenlied: Guten Abend, Gute Nacht*, which translates to "Lullaby: Good Evening, Good Night."

Brahms dedicated "Lullaby" to his friend Bertha Faber when she gave birth to her second son. Its lyrics were taken from two sources: the first stanza is from a collection of German folk poems called *Des Knaben Wunderhorn* ("The Boy's Magic Horn"), and the second stanza is by German writer Georg Scherer. The piece was premiered in 1869 by vocalist Marie Louise Dustmann-Meyer, accompanied by Clara Schumann (a composer and piano virtuoso, and wife of composer Robert Schumann).

"Brahms' Lullaby" is easily the most famous lullaby, but many other composers, including Frédéric Chopin, Maurice Ravel, Igor Stravinsky, and George Gershwin, have written famous examples.

WIEGENLIED:
GUTEN ABEND, GUTE NACHT
(Good Evening, Good Night)
(Brahms' Lullaby)

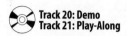
Track 20: Demo
Track 21: Play-Along

Composed by
JOHANNES BRAHMS
Arranged by BILL GALLIFORD

Gentle lullaby (♩ = 72)

Rondeau

(from *Symphonies and Fanfares for the King's Supper*)
(*Masterpiece Theatre* theme)

An early score of an opera called *Pirithoüs* by Jean-Joseph Mouret

Jean-Joseph Mouret
(1682–1738)

Jean-Joseph Mouret was one of the leading composers in France during the Baroque era. Very little of his music is performed today, but he is remembered for writing "Rondeau," which became the theme for the PBS television series *Masterpiece Theatre*.

Rondeau is the French name for *rondo*, which is a common musical form where a main theme is repeated throughout a piece with contrasting themes, called *episodes*, appearing in between. Composers have taken many different approaches to rondo form, but the most common are ABA, ABACA, and ABACABA—where "A" represents the main theme, and "B" and "C" represent episodes.

Jean-Joseph Mouret enjoyed considerable success for most of his life, but he suffered setbacks in his latter years. Mouret fell into poverty and eventually died while he was in a charitable asylum.

RONDEAU
(from *Symphonies and Fanfares for the King's Supper*)
(*Masterpiece Theatre* theme)

Composed by
JEAN-JOSEPH MOURET
Arranged by BILL GALLIFORD

Track 22: Demo
Track 23: Play-Along

molto rit.

Andante

(Second Movement from *Symphony No. 94*, "Surprise Symphony")

Franz Joseph Haydn
(1732–1809)

Austrian composer Franz Joseph Haydn made two trips to London in his career. While there, he enjoyed great success and composed a group of 12 symphonies that became known as the "London symphonies." The second of these was *Symphony No. 94 in G Major* (nicknamed the *Surprise Symphony*).

The name "Surprise Symphony" was given to the piece because of its second movement, "Andante." In it, the main theme of the piece is presented very quietly, then, suddenly, the orchestra plays a very loud chord with the timpani. The piece then goes on as though nothing had happened. This was a joke that caught the attention of the audience, and the piece was an immediate success at its premiere.

When asked years later why he wrote this "surprise" into the piece, Haydn said he wanted to give the public something new to outdo rival concerts his student Ignaz Pleyel was giving in London at the time.

ANDANTE
(Second Movement from *Symphony No. 94, "Surprise Symphony"*)

Track 24: Demo
Track 25: Play-Along

Composed by
FRANZ JOSEPH HAYDN
Arranged by BILL GALLIFORD

Henrik Klausen as Peer Gynt (1876)

Morning Mood

(from *Peer Gynt*)

Edvard Grieg
(1843–1907)

"Morning Mood" from *Peer Gynt* by Norwegian composer Edvard Grieg is one of the many well-known pieces he composed. Grieg is one of the major figures of the Romantic era and is widely recognized for the *incidental music* he wrote for *Peer Gynt*, originally a play by Norwegian dramatist Henrik Ibsen. Incidental music is intended to accompany and set the mood for an otherwise non-musical work, such as a play or today's television shows, video games, and movies. A film score is a great example of incidental music.

"Morning Mood," through continued use in television and films, has become a standard piece for evoking morning and nature. In Grieg's *Peer Gynt*, "Morning Mood" was meant to represent morning in the Moroccan desert.

Track 26: Demo
Track 27: Play-Along

MORNING MOOD
(from *Peer Gynt*)

Composed by
EDVARD GRIEG
Arranged by BILL GALLIFORD

Morning Mood - 2 - 1

Poster for an American production of Georges Bizet's *Carmen*
Created by Liebler & Maass Lith., New York (ca. 1896)

Habanera

(from *Carmen*)

Georges Bizet
(1838–1875)

One of the most popular and commonly performed operas is *Carmen* by French composer Georges Bizet. There are many memorable pieces in *Carmen*, but the tune known as "Habanera" is a true standout.

"Habanera" is the popular name for the *aria* "L'amour est un oiseau rebelle," French for "Love is a rebellious bird." An aria is a vocal solo, and "Habanera" is the first one sung by the title character, Carmen.

Sadly, Georges Bizet died very young at age 36, only a few months after *Carmen* premiered. The opera was not well-received at the time, so Bizet died thinking his opera was a hopeless failure. Of course, *Carmen* has since become one of the most famous operas in history.

HABANERA
(from *Carmen*)

Composed by
GEORGES BIZET
Arranged by BILL GALLIFORD

Habanera - 2 - 1

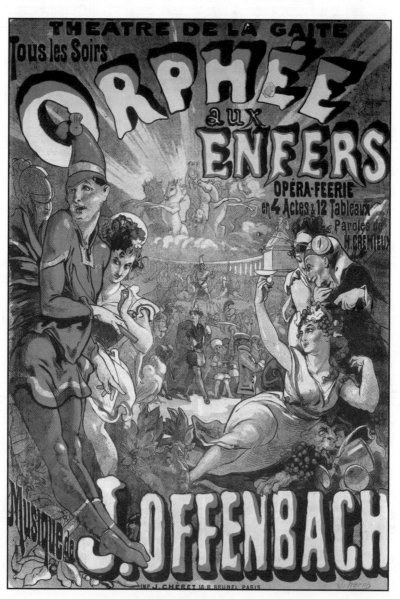

Playbill from an 1874 revival of *Orpheus in the Underworld*

Can Can

(from *Orpheus in the Underworld*)

Jacques Offenbach
(1819–1880)

German-born French composer Jacques Offenbach is best known for *Orpheus in the Underworld*, one of the most successful *operettas* (light operas) during his lifetime and to this day.

The most recognizable piece from *Orpheus in the Underworld* is "Infernal Galop," popularly and mistakenly known as "Can Can." The *can-can* is a dance that originated in the early 1800s, and Offenbach's music for this dance in *Orpheus*, "Infernal Galop," became the most famous version—so much so that Offenbach's piece came to be called "Can Can."

Offenbach was a strong influence on the operetta genre, providing inspiration for many composers after him, including the famous English duo of W. S. Gilbert and Arthur Sullivan.

Track 30: Demo
Track 31: Play-Along

CAN CAN
(from *Orpheus in the Underworld*)

Composed by
JACQUES OFFENBACH
Arranged by BILL GALLIFORD

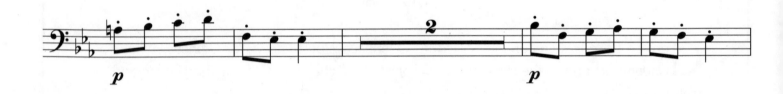

Can Can - 2 - 1

PARTS OF A TROMBONE AND POSITION CHART

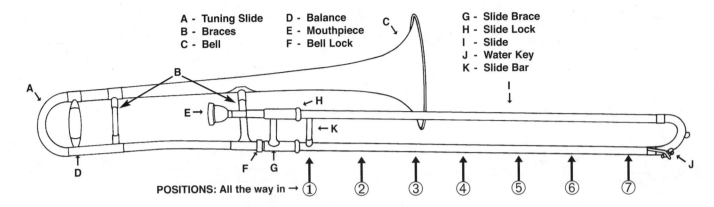

How To Read The Chart

The number of the position for each note is given in the chart below. See the picture above for the location of the slide bar for each position. When two enharmonic tones are given on the chart (F# and Gb as an example), they sound the same and are played with the same position. Alternate positions are shown underneath for trombones with a trigger (T=thumb trigger).

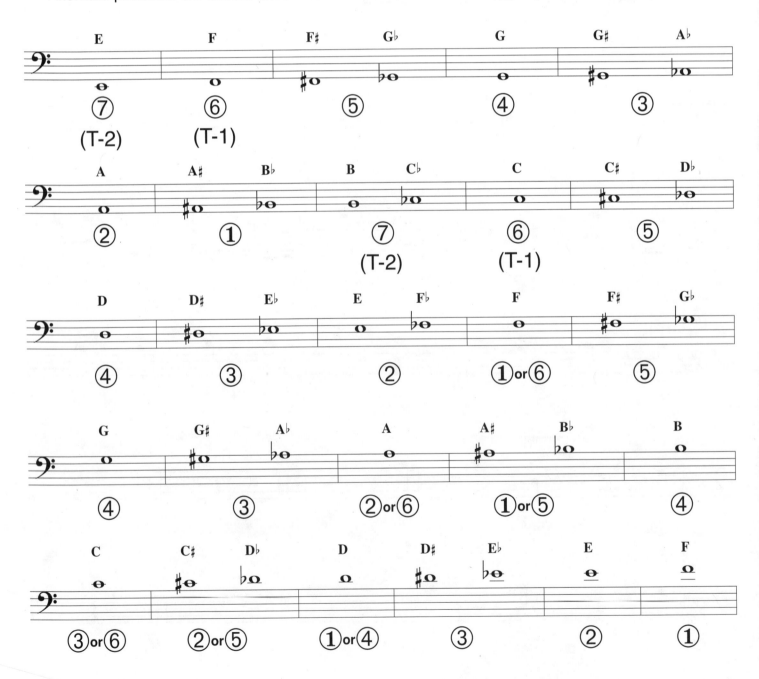